OUR LADY PEACE

OUR LADY PEACE

AND OTHER WAR POEMS, BY

MARK VAN DOREN

THE POET OF THE MONTH

NEW DIRECTIONS · NORFOLK · CONNECTICUT

OUR LADY PEACE

How far is it to peace, the piper sighed,
The solitary, sweating as he paused.
Asphalt the noon; the ravens, terrified,
Fled carrion thunder that percussion caused.

The envelope of earth was powder loud;
The taut wings shivered, driven at the sun.
The piper put his pipe away and bowed.
Not here, he said. I hunt the love-cool one,

The dancer with the clipped hair. Where is she?
We shook our heads, parting for him to pass.
Our lady was of no such trim degree,
And none of us had seen her face, alas.

She was the very ridges we must scale,
Securing the rough top. And how she smiled
Was how our strength would issue. Not to fail
Was having her, gigantic, undefiled,

For homely goddess, big as the world that burned,
Grandmother and taskmistress, field and town.
We let the stranger go; but when we turned
Our lady lived, fierce in each other's frown.

Now that the seas are limed
With fire, and a fathom under
Water spouts prepare,
In the salt cold, their thunder;

Now that the land is warm
For the due rain, for the seed,
But war birds, dropping sulphur,
Drone, and the borders bleed;

Now that the ways are strangled,
Now that the best has been,
Where lies the hidden pathway
Verity walked in?

Still hidden; as when blue peace
Clouded no other sky,
And would not name our death dates,
Nor answer how and why;

Nor happen along these pavements,
Lightening with news
The feet wherewith we stumble
Still, cursing our shoes.

Rumors of peace, rush otherwhere if policy
Stinks in your breath, if someone's advantage blows
Still so straight and so strong, so headed for somewhere.
This is no place at all, and we are no people.
Here is the wind's end, tuned to the weaker voices
Of a last victory, death words of a war.

Purposeless whisper, straggle this far if you can,
Then fail. Surrender is music here, exhaustion
Is trumpets that others will blow, standing above you
And filling the world with silver. See, we have waited
All the war years, and this one is ancient already.
Let it die with you, here where the last wind sleeps.

Not to be tricked by truces, not to be pleased
With the half brass of triumph, now we are waiting
On death words: The giants, weary, have laid themselves
    down.
Come of your own will, rumor, as sighs escape,
As humming. Nothing is lost here. Sound is reborn.
Listen. Your last is our first; is silver; is gold.

STATUS

What would I have then
Who fear the great change?
Domino centuries?
Children less strange
Then these are: identical
Lambs of the range?

What would you have,
Who implore the disaster?
Looms to be locked
When the right thing is master?
Selvage all fixed?
The coloring faster?

Neither could bear it,
Catastrophe's loss.
Look far enough,
There is nothing but moss.
We would shiver like geese,
With no graves to cross.

Rain, that wets powder,
Slows axles,
Blinds bombers,
Gurgles in grass roots too, and clover;
Steadies the knees
Of flowers, of trees
That soon will surround
A burst battleground.

Rain, that delays
Far meetings,
Fierce onsets,
Thickens the old hide, doubles the armor
Of earth, that will bleed
No more than it need
When man the newcomer
Seizes his summer.

Rain all the while
Stores noiseless
Provisions;
Tangles the meadows, jungles the woodlots;
Mixes a meal
Of rust for steel;
Is quartermaster
Against disaster.

CONQUERORS

It is a kind of love, insisting
After pursuit upon surrender;
After defeat the willing death
Of everything but woman's gender:

Woman if it is hers to dote,
Rising to receive again
The palm that felled her; were it woman's
Blood that blesses regimen.

Believing so, the angry thrust
Repeats itself; and grows more wild
As something on the ground refuses,
Red, to be with horror's child;

Bruised, to be the happy bride
Of bludgeons, of affection's fist:
Insanely falling as the man,
The woman, and the babe are missed.

THE DOOMSTERS

The difference they prophesy,
If utter, disappoints the fear;
Apprehension only starves,
Staring at too far a year:
Feeding upon too changed a woe
From any that time's children know.

If relative, a law decides:
From this to that, so many causes.
Whereupon the fear grows fat;
Then midway of its feasting pauses:
Recognition stales the fare
Sooner than panic can prepare.

Too strange, a blank; too known, a foe
Familiarity refuses.
Experience lies down with doom,
That sleeps again, as history uses.
The difference they weep and sing
Is nothing, or is everything.

How far to heroes from this spindle stretch
Of scrub that leans together, looking in:
Ostriches to storm, except for sand,
For darkness; all is upward and sun blind.

Continents of sapling save for scorn,
For promise; all atilt, all mutual pleased.
How many scuffling leagues, how many pits
Of years until the selvage of sweet wood,

Of horn, of hardness, separately old:
Oh, organ tall the harmony none hears.
Within there is but each, and each more hoarse
Than others: heaven's pillars, groaning on.

How far and deep to heroes where the touch
Is not of neighbor skins but sky and ground;
With night between, the perpendicular,
The splendid, lightning cicatriced and sound.

CYCLE

What shall be said of the lucent, the going,
Then of those that come in, swart swine from the fog;
Tooth fronted and terrible: See? their hindquarters,
Not to be seen yet, say danger is young.

Danger is young yet, but haunches will form
And hind hooves have purchase in, hard, the daylight.
What shall be said then of shoulder blades going:
There! At the boundary! The small of their backs!

Fine waisted, they opal, they burn in the sunset.
Slow they go out: after image of grace.
But, swift all the while, this breasted inbruising
Of mist hogs who froth because flanks are not free.

But they will be. Is that what is said? Is it cycle?
These in their turn to be goers, be pearl,
Be clarity fading, millenniums on,
While other forequarters, and hairy, foam through?

DEFEATIST

He is so proud, recalling
An assignation once
With Utter, and Impossible,
And him that hunts
Pure Death out where it corners
Accident for dunce.

He is so pleased, approaching
Those torturers again;
It is a second confluence
With regimen;
And last, if Chance's courage,
Dark, dies in it then.

He is so cool arriving,
This master of despair,
That he can miss the hectic
Whereat they stare:
The burning cap, in an angle
Empty except for air.

THE LITTLE WARS

The million little wars
Of peace: the sharpened word,
All night the grassy rustle,
All afternoon, absurd,

The games, the leather shouting,
The white lines to cross;
All over earth the tinkle
Of silver win and loss:

The billion little battles
Of peace are like a sea,
Are like a field that wimples,
And would eternally,

Save for the one, the War,
The hawk wing that reaches,
Suddenly, and stops
Bravest breath; and teaches

No one now to move,
No one here to mar
The death peace, the waiting
On one, the overwar

That would not have us glisten,
That loathes the little waves,
The trillion, the green trembling
Peace returns and saves.

TOTAL WAR

For the grey temples, for the slippered feet
That bounded such a life as, bent to grace,
Looks brittle now, looks breakable, the word
Nevertheless is shatter; the shocked face

Must fly on other errands, the pale shins
Must brown, must bruise themselves, and all that trunk
Be fragments; the cohesive thought be shrapnel
Peppering cold skies. The sands are sunk

That pedestalled our figure, that as one
Mock granite sounded echo to our soul;
Whose end is now this grit, these million grains
That star a blackened heaven, where no whole

Ever again may shape. Yet, gentlemen,
Be shivered. What was habit now is myth,
Is mumbling. Let it go. A huger form
Waits round the world: man still, and monolith.

What is it, not to fear?
What is it some can see
Beyond the battle's edges,
Distant, cool, and free?

It is a thing not altered
By what will happen here.
Whoever bleeds, that body
Blessed is and clear.

That person—for its wounding
Were no less grief than ours—
Keeps interval: remoter
Than Thrones, Dominions, Powers.

And cannot die; which opens
This alley to our gaze
Wheredown the foeman, startled,
Sees nothing but moon maze.

Two vessels of his heart converged in wish
For the loud hour of peace: the bells, the pounding
Of the free blood again, the ears reopened
After such hush, after such lull of sounding.

But left and right they differed; one received,
One sent the stream of longing. So, and sinister,
One hope was but for silence's cessation:
At any cost an end, though death be minister.

But the right side said no, endure it yet,
And let it be our shout that splits the quiet.
Victorious, we live to swell the singing,
And the top note is ours; nor shall we sigh it,

Sister, as now. The music to be made
Is yours and mine, so be you fresher, fatter
In courage, and tune all your strings to toughness:
Like mine, against millennium's long chatter.

Halt, commanded bombers,
Stand where you are, said the brown
Shoulders hunched and coming,
Said the hoarse throat of war.
But the world's people, balanced
On bitter feet, grew sore.

Hobbled, they heard the aching
Bones in their own arches;
Heard them angry together,
And guessed the consequence:
Some day, and soon, regardless,
The interdicted dance.

Some day, and soon, resuming,
Some day, and high, the lift
Of heel and toe, of lightfoot
Shuffle; and then the click
Of forward, backward bodies
As earth relearned to rock.

CHRISTMAS, 1941

The millions at this solstice
Who cannot see the long,
The white days coming:
To them no song

Except the death of others,
By bullet or by ice,
In dark Malayan waters
Or where the North Sea mice

Eat hawsers, and a howling
Wind from pole to pole
Brings minute word of bleeding,
Of the surrendered soul;

Of agony that nothing
Is song enough to soothe
Except of million others
The strong death news.

POND IN WARTIME

So far from sirens and the fear of wings
That fold not, so content with the one foe
Whose hunger, not whose anger, flexes plumes
And hovers: how explain it, the cold luck
That keeps five trout I know forever gliding,
Ever in weedy corners hunched and hiding?

I see them there as though the summer still
Kept green for me and warmed the vacant fields
They knew not, spreading sideward from their pool.
Nor do I have it now, the crossing land,
Nor can I bend, arriving, and count backs
To the slim fifth, the sluggard, the late born

Who dreaded me too little, and I laughed.
He would not know it now if I should name him
Lazy; no one crosses the brown stretch
And shadows winter water. Even if there
I shouted, they are dozing, the deep five:
Safer than luck interprets, and more live.

EPIDEMIC

Panic has feet to fly with, and the ground
For purchase: no lost motion as it mists
All the low lying places. It is the first
Infection, and most terrible. The bowels
Are close above, and comfort every growth.

Yet all the while another link prepares:
From head to head, solitary, the winging
Of one free thought, corruptless, with no power
To enter the sick region. It is weak
With cleanness, and with beating the white air.

Then, miracle of reason, the dry lines
It drew through lucid space become a web
That the heart loves, the strong one close below;
Which heaves to it; and hears the nether curse
At courage's contagion, no more slow.

This man kept courage when the map of fear
Was continents, was paleness to the poles,
Was Jupiter milk white, was Venus burning.
The very stones lay liquid with despair,
And the firm earth was bottomless. This man

Could walk upon that water; nay, he stamped
Till the drops gravelled, till a sound returned
Of pillars underheel, of granite growing.
This man, alone on seas, was not afraid.
So continents came back. So color widened:

Bands upon blankness. So the other men,
The millions, lifted feet and let them down;
And the soil held. So courage's cartographer,
Having his globe again, restored each mass,
Each meadow. And grasshoppers sang to him.

MYOPIA

Pity for them, the coasters
Past premonition's reef
Who then but toss and shudder
In shoals; whence their belief
That all the sea is shallow,
And only sand is grief.

Who coming near, can measure
None but the present threat;
Who do not see the high ground,
The grimmest danger yet:
The tower that must be taken
After the waves forget.

Pity for them, the tremblers
Too far away from truth
To know its drought and hardness;
Indifferent, uncouth;
And how not to have tried it
Crowns all other ruth.

Bleak order, and impromptu
Quiet; the made hush
As telephones intensely
Listen, and files flap;

As on their hooks the papers
Straighten, gravity's yawn
Relaxing the bent word:
No prisoners taken;

Smoothing to a smile,
Erroneous, the warning;
Or to disaster's placard,
Death window in a wall.

Who knows? Not they, the orderlies,
Not he, lieutenant-colonel
Of cavalry; who whistles,
Meanwhile, to far horses.

Adjutant, he sends them,
Anciently, the high cheer:
The Regiment; and taps out
Courage on a cold desk.

Most terrible the time, with nations falling
In bloody clusters, blameless. For what man
Wanted such woe? What imbeciles of might
Hunt in the heavens, torturing sweet space?

It is no time for icicles of tales
Tinkling our curiosity, for death
In little, for detective voices narrowing
Evil and good to footprints in fine snow,

To sediment in goblets. Yet it may be.
In the saved hours of Saturday, what harm
In miniatures, in frost work on one pane,
One mirror no more window to lost worlds?

For so man sees himself there, by a fire,
Preferring the old law, the immemorial
Fragment, and of those that love it still
The victory. What hurt if heaven dreams?

THE LACING

This danger that like wire
Ingathers all to one;
And every morning shortens,
Cutting in and in;

This noose about mankind's
Huge waist, that not till now
Felt bondage, or had bled
From anything but blow;

These stays that never stop,
As if an ogre pulled
Whose foothold was the moon,
The merciless, the chilled:

When will that tightness be
As nothing? Or as form
Henceforward to maintain,
To feel as grace's germ?

As closeness to be loved.
Then, when the figure clears,
A sweet incurving line,
Ageless, among stars.

HOLIDAY

For this one day much thanks, and for
Its wetness, spreading east from war
To where the rains rise, orient cool
Against the hectic. Man and fool,
I dip and splash, I tangle feet
In knots of sorrel as I greet
Pure greyness coming, on and on,
And do but think it is our dawn
Against the fever's black and red.
I drench my knees, I hunch my head,
Banishing all bruise of sound
Except this whisper, mound to mound,
Among the grass roots: "Man and child,
Woe upon him in the wild
Noon and midnight still to be;
It is not over, finding me."
Nor do I say it is the end.
Not yet, my freshener, my friend.

Stones of the street are notes for musical boys
And for their girls complaining. Manholes clank
With the running and catching up and the marching off:
Bravado. Not a youth of them but yells
Somehow the moment's meaning, blood or bells.

And age's image of them, second children
Huddled in casements, happy, their shrunk heads
Citrous with grin, tacticians of far terror:
Never an ancient there but has his day
Like a dry pebble kicked, nor canted away.

Whom the war muffles is the middle ones,
The guardians in prime. For them the peace
Longest had been laborious. What loss,
What premonition! Which is why they go
More noiseless in their anger, and more slow.

Pray never. But if no one hears,
And noise is coming, and cold tears,
What highest cornices elect
Will weep them? And does stone suspect?

Patience, quarried and set there,
So far from ground, so poor in air;
But then so proud among the gulls
And the white steam that puffs and lulls;

Patience, vain of its keen edge,
Will shatter, and some blunted ledge
Mournfully to returning birds
Will echo our own broken words.

But which up there, and who below?
And when the night? O, if you know,
Atoms elect, make loud reply.
Fate comes double if we deny.

THAT DAY

Even if wars to come sleep warm and small,
Deep seeds in action's body not yet born;
Even if horror then, sometimes the now
Looks fearfuller; is absolute forlorn;
In its own form seems final. Whence we say,
Sometimes, there is no day beyond that day,

That day of bells, of prodigal high sirens
Howling, when the harbor whistles burst
And dancers on the street take off their heads.
For the last idiot singer shall be first
On such a morning, leveller of men
With girls, and with a boy come home again.

Sometimes. And yet the germs, the little ghosts,
Still haunt us in their unmade mothers' blood.
And if we think, they grow; as time itself
Ticks in the dark, and horror in the bud
Stands giant high, a forest doomed to fall
On that day's children, armistice and all.

Our Lady Peace by Mark Van Doren has been set in Janson and Ultra-Bodoni types and printed at The Spiral Press, New York. Completed in July, 1942. Typography by Joseph Blumenthal.